WHAT THE ARTIST SAW

Henri Matisse

He saw the world in bold colour

Written by
Heather Alexander

Illustrated by
Margarida Esteves

Henri Émile Benoît Matisse was born on
31 December 1869 in Le Cateau-Cambrésis
and grew up in Bohain-en-Vermandois,
both villages in northeastern France.

Henri's father and mother ran a shop that sold seeds and hardware. Because Henri was the eldest of two brothers, he was expected to take over one day. He was not excited. He found the business boring and his town dreary. It was filled with factories that wove fabric on big looms, and their chimneys spewed thick smoke into the sky. To Henri, everything here looked and felt grey.

But his mother always brightened their cottage with colour. She covered the floors with red carpets and kept orange goldfish in bowls. She painted designs on porcelain plates that she hung on the walls.

As a child, Henri was given a few drawing lessons. The strict teachers made him copy geometric shapes and never let him use colour. Drawing like this was boring, so he stopped.

Do you like to doodle? Draw your favourite doodles.

Henri feared living a grey life like his parents and their neighbours. He wished to do something exciting when he grew up, like join a circus! When his younger brother Auguste-Emile agreed to take over the store, Henri was greatly relieved. Now he was free to do whatever he wanted . . . but he didn't know what that was. He attended law school then got a job as a law clerk. Henri found this work dull. As he read legal documents, he'd draw designs in the margins.

> "But the moment I had that paint box in my hands, I felt that this was my life."
>
> Henri Matisse

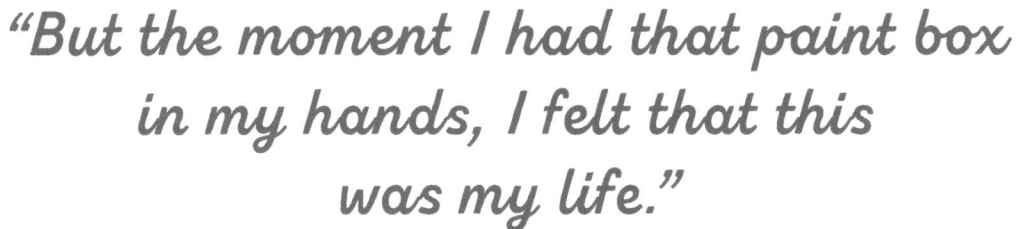

When he was 20 years old, Henri became ill with appendicitis and had to stay in hospital for a long while. The man in the bed next to him painted small landscapes to pass the time. Maybe he'd try that, too. The next day, Henri's mother brought him a set of paints, and that's when he discovered what brought him joy – painting!

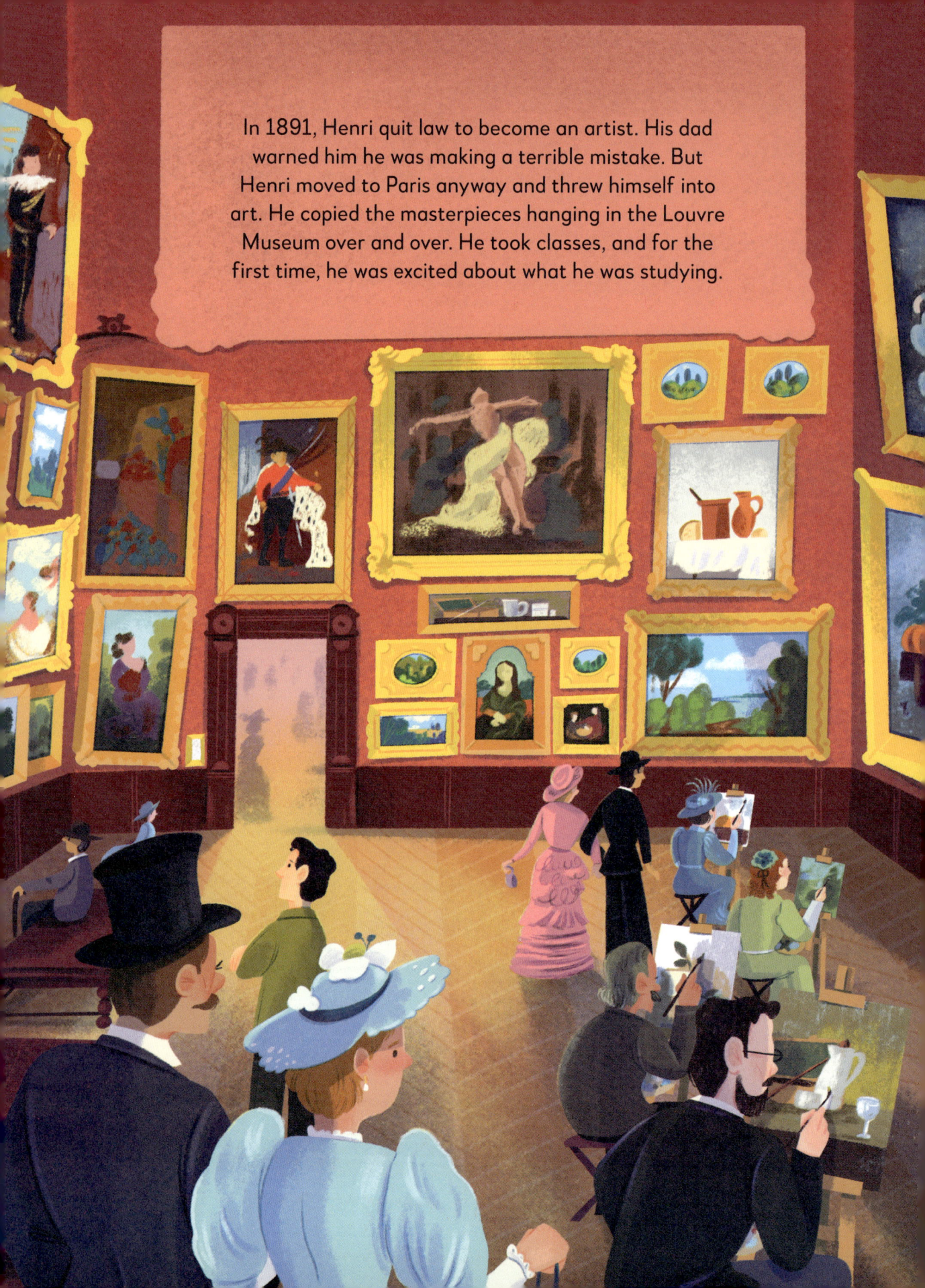

In 1891, Henri quit law to become an artist. His dad warned him he was making a terrible mistake. But Henri moved to Paris anyway and threw himself into art. He copied the masterpieces hanging in the Louvre Museum over and over. He took classes, and for the first time, he was excited about what he was studying.

Henri created still-life paintings in the traditional style. He'd paint a stack of his law books or fruit in a bowl. The objects looked realistic and were painted in dark, muted colours. But after seeing the work of French painter Paul Cézanne, Henri began to focus more on shape and colour.

Henri hoped to be admitted to École des Beaux-Arts, the best art school in Paris. He submitted drawings, but they said he was not good enough – yet. Henri worried he would never be good enough. But he kept learning and getting better, and he kept submitting his drawings.

Finally, Henri was admitted!

Henri and his artist friends would sometimes play a game as they walked about Paris with their sketchbooks. They competed to see who could capture the likeness of a person strolling by the fastest. Could they convey in a single brushstroke what made that person special?

Try it with words! In one word, describe what makes your pet or your bedroom or your favourite outfit special.

While in art school, Henri painted more still lifes and many landscapes. When he was introduced to the work of Post-Impressionist painters, such as Vincent van Gogh, he began to move away from dark colours.

In 1898, Henri married Amélie Parayre, who ran a hat shop in Paris. When they met, Henri was a struggling artist who had never sold a painting, but Amélie believed in him. She worked long hours to support Henri's dream, and she often modelled for him, too. Together, they raised three children: Marguerite, Jean, and Pierre.

During the summer of 1905, Henri moved his family to Collioure, a small fishing port on the Mediterranean Sea. Another French artist, André Derain, joined them. Henri and André were amazed by all the dazzling colour. Flowers bloomed in rainbow hues. Leafy trees dripped with ripe oranges, lemons, and figs. Brilliant sunlight made the blue bay sparkle.

Each day the two painters walked the beaches and the forests in search of the perfect place to set their easels.

Henri and André let inspiration from nature and their emotions guide them. Their paint brushes began to move more freely across the canvas. Brushstrokes ran into one another, growing looser and more spontaneous. As the weeks passed, Henri's art became more abstract and expressive.

Henri experimented with pure colour directly from the tube. He chose colours that expressed his feelings and the sensations he got from an object. A tree trunk could be orange, and water could be purple. He wasn't afraid to use unrealistic colours.

"...when I apply green, that does not mean grass. When I apply blue, that does not mean sky."

Henri Matisse

With colour alone, Henri was able to create shape, shadows, and movement.
To capture light and sunshine, he let the white canvas peek through.

What **colour** would you choose to show **happiness**?
How about **curiosity** or **wonder**?

When Henri and André returned to Paris, they exhibited their new art at the Salon d'Automne. Critics and viewers were shocked and outraged. Some even laughed when they saw Henri's painting *Woman in a Hat*. They called the portrait of his wife "hideous". They wanted to know: why had Henri used so many bright colours? And why had he put green on Amélie's face and given her blue cheeks?

Henri's painting was very different from the other art. Those paintings were done in earth tones and showed figures and objects as they looked in real life. No one had ever dared to use colour like Henri had.

The art critic and writer Louis Vauxcelles named this new, bold, colourful style Fauvism. In French, "fauve" means "wild beast". Henri was called "chief Fauve", but he didn't care. He would continue to paint the world the way he saw and felt it.

Do you have a friend who encourages or challenges you to do better? Draw a picture showing the two of you together.

Leo and Gertrude Stein, brother-and-sister art collectors from the United States, bought *Woman in a Hat*. They recognized Henri was changing the way the world thought about colour, and this gave him confidence.

On Saturdays, the Steins would invite painters and writers to their home in Paris to share ideas. These gatherings were called "salons". The Steins introduced Henri to a young Spanish artist named Pablo Picasso.

At first, Henri and Pablo shared inspiration and techniques. They even gifted each other paintings. But their relationship soon turned competitive. Henri later explained it was less a rivalry and more like a boxing match, because they were constantly challenged to do their best.

Eventually, Henri and Pablo became lifelong friends with great respect and admiration for each other.

Henri travelled widely. On trips to Morocco, he admired the abstract shape of the human figures in the wood carvings and sculptures he saw in the markets.

He began to include thick outlines and angular bodies in his work.

What do you like to do to relax?

As well as paintings and drawings, Henri created sculptures. Modelling a figure with clay could help him to puzzle out the composition of a painting, or where to position everything on a canvas. Henri also turned to sculpture for inspiration when he doubted his talent. Often worried he wasn't good enough, he'd sometimes be unable to paint. But sculpting clay with his hands helped Henri regain his focus and confidence.

By this point, Henri had moved away from the Fauve style.
He concentrated on simple forms against flat stretches of pure colour.

*What do you like to collect?
Draw your favourite object in your collection.*

He also began using pattern more. Having grown up in a town famous for weaving beautiful textiles, he liked to collect interesting fabrics from junk shops and markets. He brought back pieces with interesting geometric patterns from his many trips. Whenever he needed inspiration, Henri looked through his textile library.

Take a walk outside with your sketchbook. Draw the patterns you see in nature.

In his early paintings, patterns appeared in the background, perhaps on a tablecloth. Now the repeating decorative shapes took up more space on the canvas. He added patterns on walls and objects, too.

Sergei Shchukin, a Russian cloth merchant and a big fan of French modern art, purchased about 40 of Henri's paintings to hang in his house in Moscow. Finally, Henri was making a good living doing what he loved.

Sergei commissioned Henri to paint three works to decorate his mansion. They could be of anything the artist wanted. For one painting, Henri chose his own art studio.

The Red Studio was one of the first monochromatic works of modern art. Henri covered about two-thirds of the canvas in one colour – a deep red. Outlines showed furniture, doors, and windows but there was no depth, no shadows, and no perspective. Everything was intentionally flattened. Henri didn't worry about making objects look realistic. He felt the artist was not meant to be a camera.

What would you choose to paint?

Sergei did not like the painting and refused to take it. Years later, its greatness would be celebrated and would inspire Abstract artists, such as Mark Rothko and Ellsworth Kelly.

In 1930, an American collector named Dr Albert Barnes asked Henri to create an artwork for his Pennsylvania mansion. Henri chose simple figures dancing. He wanted the dancers to look as if they were leaping off the canvas. His strong lines would guide the viewer's eyes to create a sense of movement and joy.

But Henri had a problem. He liked to make changes while he created. He liked to try out different colours or shapes. This was fine on a small canvas but would be impossible in a space this huge. Back in France, Henri came up with a solution. He made huge coloured-paper cutouts of the figures. He pinned them to the wall and moved them about to determine where each fitted best. When satisfied, he traced them onto three large canvases and started painting.

Except when he was almost done, Henri discovered he had been using the wrong measurements! His paintings were too narrow for the space, and he had to begin all over again.

Around 1940, at age 71, Henri had a series of operations for cancer, and his poor health made it difficult for him to stand at his easel. Did Henri stop doing what he loved? No! He made art lying in bed or sitting in his wheelchair.

Henri turned to collage. His assistants painted sheets of paper in bold colours. With scissors, he cut the paper into simple curved shapes and spirals. He never used a pencil to trace the designs. Instead, he let his scissors guide his creativity. He described it as "drawing with scissors" and "cutting into colour".

Henri arranged his paper cutouts into designs or compositions. For small works, he pinned the cutouts on a board. Then he moved them about, over and over again, until he was happy with the balance of colours and shapes. For larger works that took up an entire wall in his studio, he used a long stick to position the cutouts.

Once more, Henri amazed the art world, this time with his dynamic cutouts. While they looked simple, creating them was very involved.

From paper, he snipped plants, flowers, animals, and swirly designs. Shapes in different sizes were repeated. In doing this, he created a pattern.

He placed complementary colours alongside each other. The contrast made the colours stand out and appear even brighter.

Henri played with positive and negative space. He created harmony between the two, making sure the negative space was as interesting as the positive space. In some of his works, it's tricky to pick out the positive shapes from the negative ones.

On 3 November 1954, Henri died of a heart attack at the age of 84. He made art until the day he died.

Henri Matisse helped to usher in the modern art movement with his daring use of brilliant colour, decorative patterns, and flattened space. Over his 60-year career, he experimented with many styles, but his goal was always to discover "the essential character of things" and to convey joy. His art now hangs in museums all over the world, bringing colour into the lives of millions.

"An artist is an explorer."

Henri Matisse

Timeline of key artworks

During his career, Henri Matisse created many still-life paintings, portraits, and landscapes using bold dabs of colour and unconventional techniques. Here are a few of his key works of art that feature his spectacular style.

1899
Still Life, Compote, Apples, and Oranges

1905
Open Window, Collioure

1905
Woman with a Hat

1906
The Young Sailor II

"It has bothered me all my life that I do not paint like everybody else."

Henri Matisse

1911
The Red Studio

Timeline continued

1912
Goldfish

1912
Nasturtiums with
the Dance II

1946
Icarus

1947
The Horse, the Rider and the Clown

1953
The Sheaf

Painting with feeling

Henri Matisse believed that an artist shouldn't just copy the appearance of an object but should portray how that object makes them feel. He accomplished this through colour. He purposefully chose hues that captured his intense emotions, even if those colours were not realistic.

1899
Still Life, Compote,
Apples, and Oranges

Let your emotions guide you as you create a still life. You can work with paint, marker pens, crayons, or colouring pencils.

Start by gathering a variety of fruits and vegetables. Arrange them on a plate or in a bowl.

Begin drawing the fruit or vegetables in the front and work your way backwards. Concentrate on the basic shapes and different sizes. You don't need every detail.

Challenge yourself!

Your turn!

Take your time. Unlike people or animals, objects don't move!

Now fill in your drawing with bold colour. Experiment with unrealistic colours. Maybe use black to outline the objects, like Henri often did.

Not into fruit? Try a still life of flowers in a vase, crayons in a mug, a stack of your favourite books, a small toy, or your sleeping pet.

"I do not literally paint that table, but the emotion it produces upon me."

Henri Matisse

Draw with scissors

Cutout collages may look simple but arranging the different pieces and colours to create a dynamic and balanced composition can be quite tricky.

1953
The Sheaf

First, choose four or five different colours of construction paper that you feel go together.

With an adult's help, use scissors to cut a variety of shapes directly into the paper like Henri did.

Gather your shapes in a pile. Save your negative shapes as well as your positive ones.

"My paintings consist of four or five colours that clash with one another expressively."

Henri Matisse

Cut and paste!

When you have all your shapes, start placing them a larger sheet of paper. Don't glue them down yet; this way you can experiment with different compositions. You can overlap your shapes, placing smaller ones on top of larger ones. You do not need to use every shape you cut – only the ones that work best with your picture.

Step back and consider your work. Do you want to rearrange something? Look from top to bottom and from side to side. Are your positive and negative spaces balanced? Take your time. Henri sometimes took years on a single collage!

When you are satisfied, glue all the shapes into place. Now give your collage a title.

Try this yourself!

Glossary

Abstract
Art that does not represent real things. It uses colours, lines, and shapes to make images that express feelings.

Balance
The arrangement of elements in an artwork to make everything appear equally important.

Commission
When an artist is paid to make an artwork for a person, gallery, or museum.

Complementary colours
Colours opposite one another on the colour wheel, such as yellow/violet, blue/orange, and red/green. When they are paired together, they create a high contrast.

Composition
How images are organized on an artwork.

Fauvism
An art movement from about 1905–1910 that was known for bold colours and expressive brush strokes.

Landscape
Art that depicts the natural world.

Modern Art
A style and period of art between the late 19th and the mid-20th century that rejected traditional techniques of the past in the spirit of experimentation.

Mural
A painting or other work of art created directly on a wall.

Monochromatic
Using only one colour.

Pattern
A repeated decorative design.

Portrait
A painting or drawing of a person or animal.

Positive and Negative space
Positive space is the solid shape or form. Negative space is the empty area surrounding a shape or form.

Still Life
A painting or drawing of an arrangement of objects, such as a stack of books or fruit in a bowl.

Margarida Esteves

Margarida Esteves is an illustrator based in South London. Working primarily digitally, her work often features bold and bright colours, intricate details and rich textures. Maps, landscapes, and ballet dancers are among her favourite subjects to draw. She feels inspired by people, films, vintage illustration, and history – history holds a special place in her heart!

Beyond illustration, she enjoys writing stories and experimenting with design, typography, embroidery, and printmaking, creating small projects in the sketchbook she always carries.

Heather Alexander

Heather Alexander loves to write about art, mythology, science, and history and has written numerous books, both nonfiction and fiction, for children. When she was a child, her mother would take her on special trips into New York City to visit the art museums, and she remembers being captivated by Henri Matisse's colourful cutouts. Heather now lives in Los Angeles with her husband and beagle and is always doodling on all her papers.

Acquisitions Project Editor Sara Forster
Editor Vicky Armstrong
Project Art Editor Stefan Georgiou
Design Assistant Molly Kellond
Production Editor Siu Yin Chan
Senior Production Controller Louise Minihane
Senior Acquisitions Editor Katy Flint
Design Manager Vicky Short
Art Director Charlotte Coulais
Publishing Director Mark Searle

Art Directed and Designed by Clare Baggaley
Text by Heather Alexander
Illustrations by Margarida Esteves

First published in Great Britain in 2025 by
Dorling Kindersley Limited
20 Vauxhall Bridge Road,
London SW1V 2SA

The authorised representative in the EEA is
Dorling Kindersley Verlag GmbH. Arnulfstr. 124,
80636 Munich, Germany

Page design copyright © 2025 Dorling Kindersley Limited
A Penguin Random House Company
10 9 8 7 6 5 4 3 2 1
001–344969–Aug/2025

All rights reserved.
No part of this publication may be reproduced, stored in or introduced into a retrieval system, or transmitted, in any form, or by any means (electronic, mechanical, photocopying, recording, or otherwise), without the prior written permission of the copyright owner.
DK values and supports copyright. Thank you for respecting intellectual property laws by not reproducing, scanning or distributing any part of this publication by any means without permission. By purchasing an authorised edition, you are supporting writers and artists and enabling DK to continue to publish books that inform and inspire readers. No part of this publication may be used or reproduced in any manner for the purpose of training artificial intelligence technologies or systems. In accordance with Article 4(3) of the DSM Directive 2019/790, DK expressly reserves this work from the text and data mining exception.

A CIP catalogue record for this book
is available from the British Library.
ISBN: 978-0-2417-1715-8

Printed and bound in China

Acknowledgments
DK would like to thank Ruth Millington for fact-checking; Lisa Davis for proofreading and Martin Copeland and Geetam Biswas for picture research.

www.dk.com

Picture credits

The publisher would like to thank the following for their kind permission to reproduce their photographs:

(Key: a-above; b-below/bottom; c-centre; f-far; l-left; r-right; t-top)

37 Bridgeman Images: *Still Life, Compote, Apples, and Oranges,* 1899, Baltimore Museum of Art / © Succession H. Matisse / DACS 2024 (cla); *Woman with a Hat,* 1905, San Francisco Museum of Modern Art / © Succession H. Matisse / DACS 2024 (clb). **Image Courtesy National Gallery Of Art, Washington:** *Open Window, Collioure, 1905,* Collection of Mr. and Mrs. John Hay Whitney / © Succession H. Matisse / DACS 2024 (cra). **Photo Scala, Florence:** *The Young Sailor II, 1906,* image copyright The Metropolitan Museum of Art / Art Resource / © Succession H. Matisse / DACS 2024 (crb). **38 Photo Scala, Florence:** *The Red Studio, 1911,* The Museum of Modern Art, New York / © Succession H. Matisse / DACS 2024. **39 Archives Henri Matisse** (all rights reserved): *Nasturtiums with 'The Dance' II,* 1912, © Succession H. Matisse / DACS 2024 (l); *The Goldfish,* 1912, © Succession H. Matisse / DACS 2024 (r). **40 Archives Henri Matisse** (all rights reserved): *Icarus,* plate VIII from the illustrated book, Jazz, published 1947, © Succession H. Matisse / DACS 2024 (tl); *The Horse, the Rider, and the Clown,* plate V from the illustrated book Jazz, published 1947, © Succession H. Matisse / DACS 2024 (tr). **Photo Scala, Florence:** *The Sheaf,* 1953, Museum Associates / LACMA / Art Resource NY / © Succession H. Matisse / DACS 2024 (b). **41 Bridgeman Images:** *Still Life, Compote, Apples, and Oranges, 1899,* Baltimore Museum of Art / © Succession H. Matisse / DACS 2024 (cl). **43 Photo Scala, Florence:** *The Sheaf,* 1953, Museum Associates / LACMA / Art Resource NY / © Succession H. Matisse / DACS 2024 (cla)

All other images © Dorling Kindersley
For further information see: www.dkimages.com